LET'S EXPLORE AUSTRALIA

(MOST FAMOUS ATTRACTIONS IN AUSTRALIA)

SPEEDY
PUBLISHING

Speedy Publishing LLC
40 E. Main St. #1156
Newark, DE 19711
www.speedypublishing.com

Australia is a developed country and one of the wealthiest in the world. Australia is also a land of spectacular beauty.

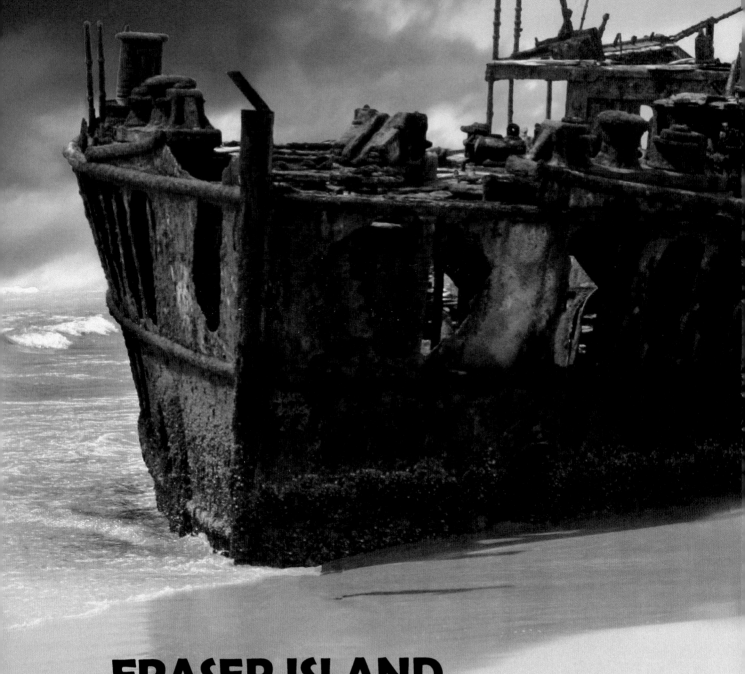

FRASER ISLAND

Is one of the most popular islands in Australia. Fraser contains rainforest that grows in sand – something unique only to this location. Fraser Island is the largest sand island in the world.

RIVER TORRENS

Is the most significant river of the Adelaide Plains and was one of the reasons for the siting of the city of Adelaide. The River Torrens divides the city centre from North Adelaide.

GOLD COAST

s a coastal city in southeastern Queensland on the east coast of Australia. Gold Coast is the most popular tourist destination in Queensland.

SYDNEY HARBOUR BRIDGE

Is a steel through arch bridge across Sydney Harbour. The dramatic view of the bridge, the harbour, and the nearby Sydney Opera House is an iconic image of Sydney, and Australia.

PORT DOUGLAS

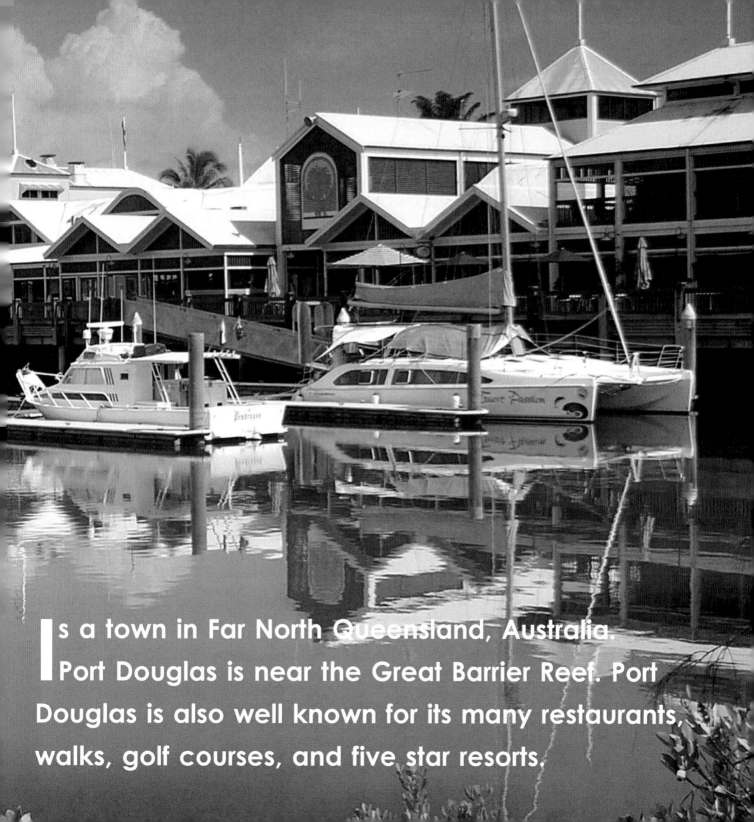

Is a town in Far North Queensland, Australia. Port Douglas is near the Great Barrier Reef. Port Douglas is also well known for its many restaurants, walks, golf courses, and five star resorts.

KANGAROO ISLAND

Is one of South Australia's most popular tourist attractions. Kangaroo Island is well known for its nature and wildlife.

KAKADU NATIONAL PARK

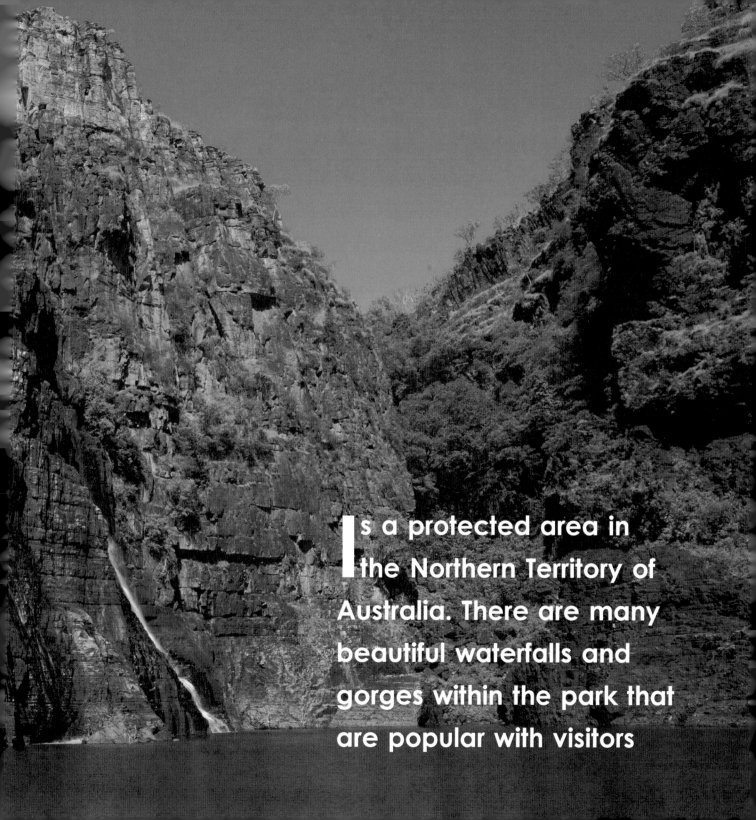

Is a protected area in the Northern Territory of Australia. There are many beautiful waterfalls and gorges within the park that are popular with visitors

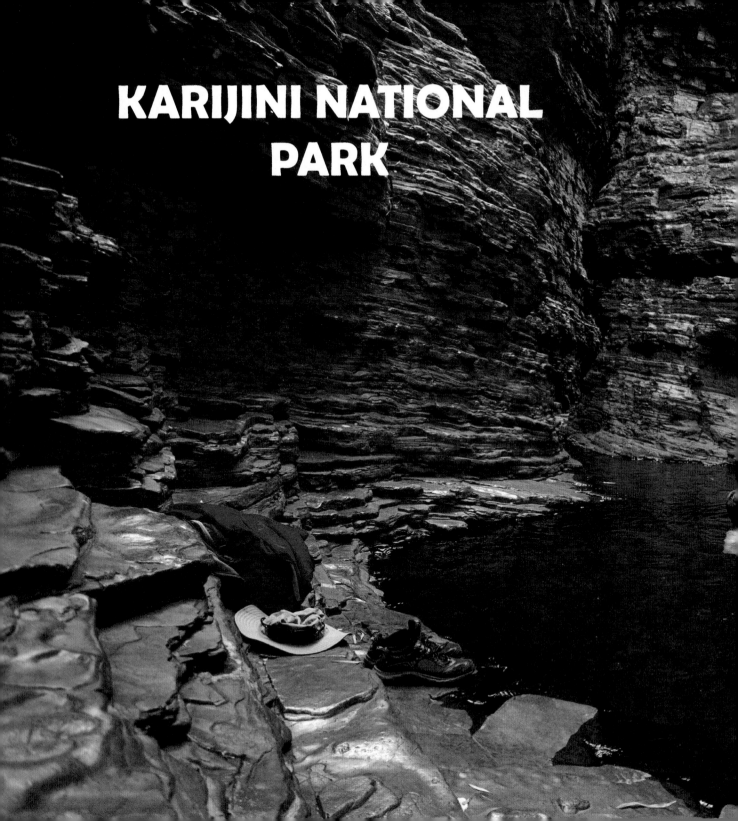

KARIJINI NATIONAL PARK

Is the second largest national park in Western Australia. The park is most notable for its four prominent gorges marked by waterfalls and water holes.

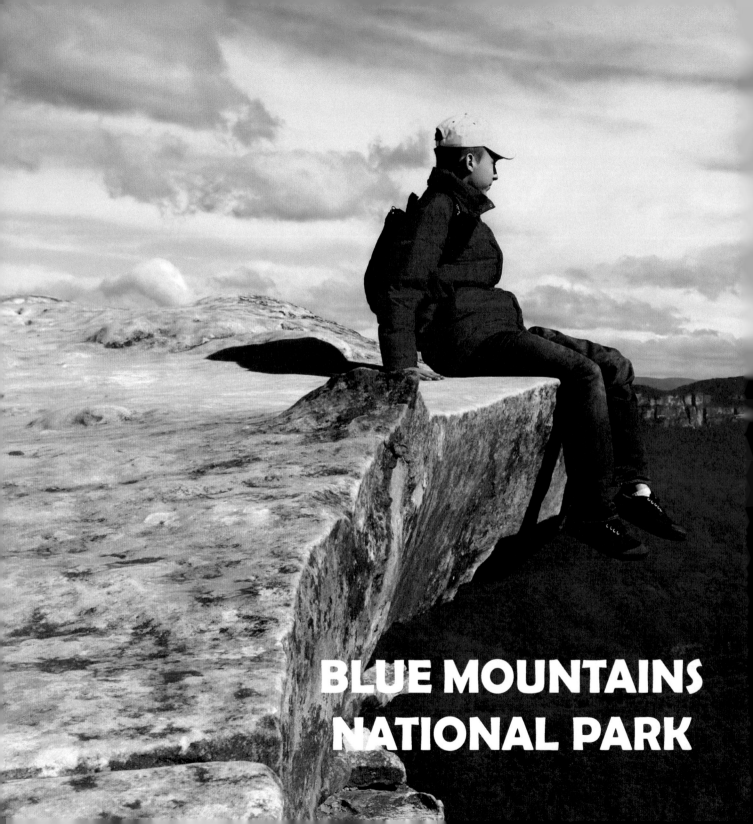

BLUE MOUNTAINS NATIONAL PARK

Is a protected national park that is located in the Blue Mountains region of New South Wales. The most famous attractions in the park are the towering sandstone rock formations called the Three Sisters.

BROOME

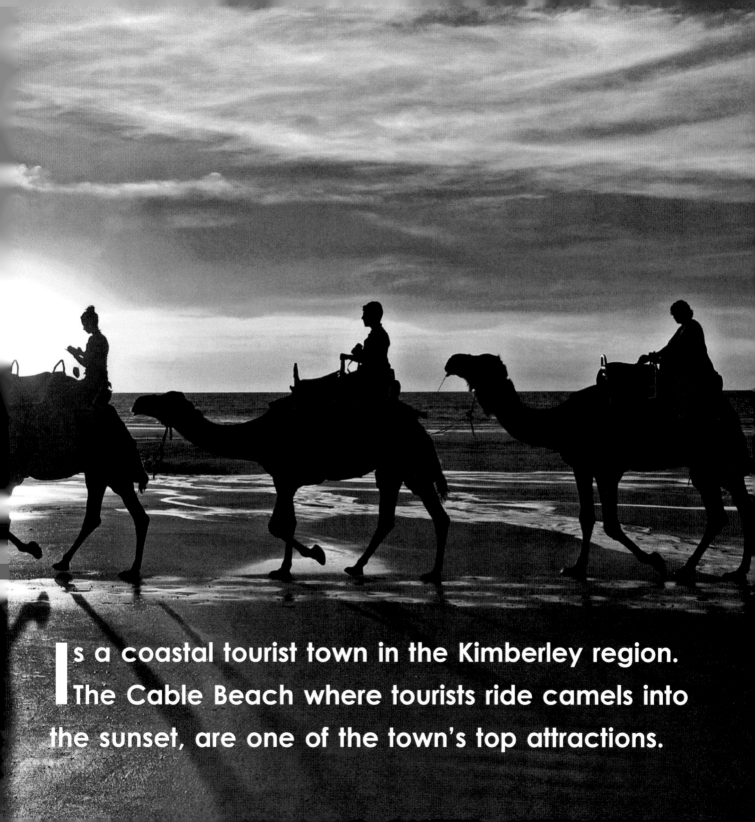

Is a coastal tourist town in the Kimberley region. The Cable Beach where tourists ride camels into the sunset, are one of the town's top attractions.

ULURU

Is one of the world's largest monoliths. One of the rock's peculiarities is that it changes colors dramatically at sunset from terra cotta to blue, violet and red.

CANBERRA

Is the capital city of Australia. Canberra is one of the most beautiful, cleanest, secure and hospitable capital cities in the world.

MELBOURNE

Is the most populous city in the Australian state of Victoria. Melbourne is considered Australia's unofficial sporting capital.

DARWIN WHARF
PRECINCT

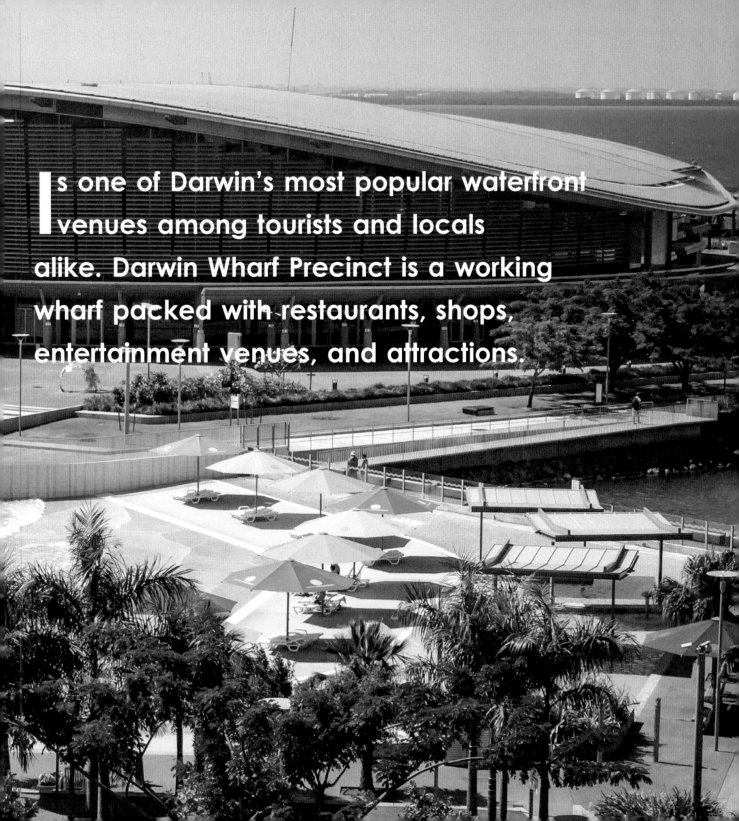

Is one of Darwin's most popular waterfront venues among tourists and locals alike. Darwin Wharf Precinct is a working wharf packed with restaurants, shops, entertainment venues, and attractions.

Made in the USA
Las Vegas, NV
05 March 2023

68578012R00021